HILDEGARD NIEMANN

Games and House Design for
Parakeets

BARRON'S

Contents

The lively parakeets' world is just as varied as their plumage.

What Parakeets Are Like

A Dream Home for Parakeets

Keeping Parakeets Busy

The Little School for Parakeets

Tricks for Parakeets

IINSIDE EVERY CURIOUS PARAKEET BEATS
THE HEART OF A LITTLE EXPLORER!

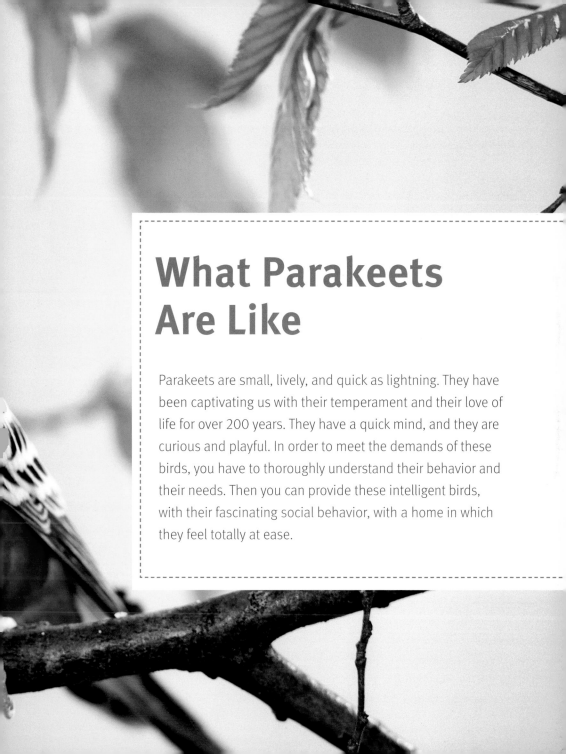

What Parakeets Are Like

Parakeets are small, lively, and quick as lightning. They have been captivating us with their temperament and their love of life for over 200 years. They have a quick mind, and they are curious and playful. In order to meet the demands of these birds, you have to thoroughly understand their behavior and their needs. Then you can provide these intelligent birds, with their fascinating social behavior, with a home in which they feel totally at ease.

Biology

In the wild, parakeets have adapted to a very extreme habitat. It is not only their physical structure, but also their overall social behavior that serves just one goal: to survive even under the most adverse conditions and stay in touch with the flock.

ALERT PREY ANIMALS

The Aborigines call parakeets "budgerigar." This means *good food*. Parakeets are prey and flight animals and are always on the lookout for enemies. Their eyes are located on the sides of their heads and provide a nearly 360-degree field of view. Parakeets react up to seven times faster than we do; this guarantees their survival if they are attacked by raptors or reptiles.

DILIGENT BREEDERS

Under good conditions, parakeets rear many young in a very short time. The little ones are fledged at four weeks and are capable of reproduction at around two months.

LONG-DISTANCE FLIERS

Even though they are so dainty, parakeets are little high-performance athletes. In the search for food, if necessary, they fly up to 61 miles (100 km) at a time before landing from exhaustion. Fat that the birds store in the breast area makes this huge feat possible.

CLEVER SURVIVALISTS

As nomads, parakeets adapt even to unaccustomed, new food sources. American buffalo grass, which was introduced from Australia, simplifies their life and provides for small, stable populations that no longer need to travel in search of food.

WELL ADAPTED

In the wild, parakeets live in very austere, dry areas. Thanks to a gland that removes salt, they can even drink water from salt lakes. And in a flock, it is easier for them to discover possible food sources.

Behaviors

A parakeet's day is a very active one, alternating between relaxing, busy goings-on, and contact with other birds in the flock. In a habitat set up like the wild, the birds never get bored.

RUBBING AND COOING

Parakeets express their devotion through mutual pushing and rubbing with their beaks. In the process, their pupils become smaller and the feathers on their heads are raised.

REGULAR REST

A little break does a lot of good. The parakeet sits relaxed on one leg and observes its surroundings. The feathers are slightly fluffed, and the feathers on the cheeks are slightly pushed forward. Often you can also hear a low grinding of the beak, a sign of well being. After an exciting morning, the birds often withdraw for a fairly long break around midday and search for a quiet, slightly elevated place for their noontime rest.

METICULOUS PLUMAGE CARE

A parakeet can fly properly only when its feathers are in perfect condition. It cleans every feather carefully with its beak and puts it into place. Energetic shaking rounds out the daily care.

ZESTFUL GNAWING

The parakeet's beak consists of keratin and grows throughout the bird's life. Every day the birds must wear away a quarter inch (6 mm) or more by gnawing. In addition to fresh twigs, they also chew up pasteboard, paper, and cardboard. If they don't have appropriate gnawing material, the birds feel out of sorts and gnaw on inappropriate things. As a result, they may suffer from poisoning.

EXUBERANT FROLICKING

Spontaneous outbreaks of *joie de vivre* from parakeets are routine. During free flight, parakeets fly while calling loudly and performing daredevil maneuvers.

Body Language

Parakeets are social creatures, and feel safe and secure only in a group. In order to live as harmoniously as possible in such a large community, the birds have developed a sophisticated body language.

↑ ANXIOUS

The parakeet stands erect on both legs. Its plumage is tight to the body, and it looks to both sides and overhead by tipping its head to the side. Shortly before taking flight, it leaves a dropping to lighten itself. When parakeets become frightened, these physical signals appear very quickly and are scarcely visible to the owner. It suddenly flies off in a frenzy or a panic. Try to figure out the cause for the fearful reaction.

TOTALLY RELAXED

The parakeet is watching but not taking part in the happenings. The feathers are tight to the body, and the bird sits on both legs. Maybe a companion can motivate it to play!

INTENSE CONCENTRATION

The parakeet is playing intently and hardly reacts when spoken to. Once something captures its attention, you can hardly distract the bird. The best thing to do is to let it continue playing.

AGGRESSIVE

Sometimes there are arguments even among parakeets. The opponents face each other with wide-open beaks and raised feet. Females especially express their displeasure through little attacks. These quarrels should not be underestimated, for the defeated bird could remain unhappy for a long time.

DURING COURTSHIP

The males warble—that is, sing, excitedly to the females with their plumage fluffed up. The female sits before the male in a slight crouch and enjoys the performance. Once things are settled, the male is allowed to mate.

Intelligence

Parakeets have to cover great distances in their search for water and food, and they continually deal with new situations. This requires a considerable amount of intelligence. The following characteristics show how smart and clever these birds are.

MIMICKRY

Parakeets continually adopt the sounds from their surroundings into their repertoire. In practicing, it is best to avoid words containing the letters "p" and "b" because parakeets really can't make these sounds.

PLAYING

Playing is a sign of intelligence, for it affords an opportunity to practice social and mental skills. Parakeets enjoy playing with colorful toys, especially if they also make noise. In addition, these jaunty fliers love wild flight games with their companions. Even swinging and climbing with friends is great fun for the birds.

CURIOSITY

Parakeets observe their surroundings very closely. Nothing escapes their sharp gaze, and they want to satisfy their curiosity quickly. If the owner is busy doing something, they think he or she must be doing something quite interesting!

APTITUDE FOR LEARNING

In contrast to song birds (exception: corvids), parakeets are capable of learning throughout their lives—and that can mean a good fifteen years! Even old birds can accomplish amazing things and appreciate new stimuli.

AMBITION

"What's in it for me?" Parakeets can display amazing ambition when they pursue a goal. Tasty food in particular motivates the birds and allows them to be at their best. They even master tricky food dispensers in the blink of an eye.

THE ATOM BALL IS A GREAT LANDING PLACE FOR THIS THREESOME OF PARAKEETS!

A Dream Home for Parakeets

The cage and aviary are our parakeets' playground. The larger and more varied this space is, the happier the birds are. Great ideas for creating the parakeets' living quarters are thought up by innovative thinking from their owners.

From Apartment to Luxury Suite

Flying, playing, climbing, seesawing: this cage, with all its variety, fulfills every parakeet's dream.

Parakeets are cheerful birds that have a great need for exercise. The daily free flight is therefore a must for these little birds. Of course, feisty parakeets mustn't be allowed to fly around in the house without supervision, for the danger of injury would be too great. Also, it is advised that you clip the wings of your birds to limit their ability to fly at full speed and, thus, potentially suffer injury. Since parakeets spend a part of the day in their cages or in an aviary, this habitat must be as well adapted as possible to the requirements of these feathered mini-athletes. It is not only the size, but also the shape of the cage or aviary that is a decisive factor in whether or not the parakeets feel comfortable in their homes.

Small but Nice: Cages

Having a small home is no obstacle to owning these energetic sprites. There are some very nice cages that accommodate the birds' needs. When you buy a cage, make sure that its width is greater than its length, for parakeets fly more horizontally than vertically. So the wider the cage, the better the birds can utilize the available space. In very dark homes, you should choose sand-colored or very light-colored, powder-coated cages, for otherwise the parakeets will sit in their cages in the dark. In bright homes, it is a good idea to choose darker models so that the wire mesh does not create glare. Also make sure that the door is large enough. Doors that are too small are unpleasant for the birds, and they may refuse to go back into the cage after their daily free flight. In addition, it is harder to take care of and set up a cage with a small door.

CAGES WITH PLUS POINTS

Many models of cages come with flaps or upper parts that swing out or flip up. In restricted space, these flaps serve as an outside perch, but they need to be equipped with some toys.

Many cages come with a mesh floor. This is intended to keep the birds from walking through their droppings when they play on the floor inside the cage. Since parakeets like to search for food on the floor, you must leave this grating in the cage and wipe it off every day with a damp cloth to prevent bacterial infections.

Roomy Aviaries

If you want to give your feathered comrades more room, or if you want to keep a small flock of parakeets, even a large cage is not adequate, for the birds need even more space. In this case, you are advised to buy an indoor aviary. There are many suppliers that market ready-made aviaries in all sizes and shapes, as well as individual aviary modules. With many options available, you can set up an aviary that is adapted individually to your living situation.

- For fairly small homes, pentagon-shaped corner aviaries are a good choice (see photo, page 14). They save space in the room and offer the birds enough space, as long as they have time for their daily free flight.
- Large, luxurious aviaries can even be placed in the corner of a room. The birds can fly for short distances and must maneuver around the curves.
- If the aviary is at least 80 inches long by 40 inches wide by 80 inches high (200 × 100 × 200 cm), you can even occasionally omit the free flight for the birds if you don't have time to supervise.
- Parakeets will feel right at home in an aviary that is 80 inches by 40 inches by 80 inches (200 × 100 × 200 cm). With every additional square yard or meter of surface area, you can add another pair of birds. If the birds have free flight every day, you can put in another pair.

This aviary is so large that it can be a home to a small flock of parakeets.

A PROPER SETUP: THE BASICS

When you buy an aviary, you should make sure that the wire used is not galvanized, for parakeets often like to climb on the wire and nibble it. With galvanized mesh, there is a danger of heavy metal poisoning. It costs a little more to buy aluminum mesh, but in the long run it is better for your parakeet's health. The mesh size should not exceed a half inch (1.25 cm), for otherwise very small birds could force their heads through the wire and get stuck.

Floor and Bedding: It is best to cover the floor of an indoor aviary with beech wood shavings from a pet shop. Scatter the shavings under the perches daily, for the birds search for food in the bedding and keep coming into contact with their droppings. Once a week, you should change the bed-

> ## Tip
>
> Get an aviary with wheels. These can be moved around easily for cleaning. If the aviary is placed right against a wall, it should be painted with an environmentally friendly, **water-resistant** paint before the birds are put inside so that the wall is easy to clean.

ding, for it becomes moist from urine and atmospheric humidity, and mildew could form. An alternative is plain white paper tablecloths that can be easily changed in the evening. Put in some bowls filled with sand so that the parakeets can still satisfy their need to search for food on the floor, but don't place the bowls beneath the perches or droppings will fall into them.

Food Trays: In indoor aviaries, food is provided in trays. These trays pivot and make it possible to change the dishes quickly, because owners can simply rotate them out without having to open the aviary door. The dishes usually are made of metal and are easy to clean.

Private Space: You should have a dividing wall between the aviary and your living area

Not much space but lots of room: A fancifully arranged corner aviary is the perfect solution for small homes.

In aviaries built in a corner, parakeets can even perform nimble flight maneuvers.

so that the parakeets can rest at night. One good possibility is curtains attached to a strip of wood that can be placed in front of the aviary at night. During the day, the curtain must be pulled securely to the side so that the parakeets don't use it as a toy.

The Right Location

Even the location of the cage and aviary determines whether or not the parakeets feel comfortable in their home. Make sure that the birds are not exposed to direct sunlight. Parakeets must also have the opportunity to stay in the shade during the summer. If the aviary is placed in a very noisy place—for example, next to a door—put some plants that are not poisonous to parakeets in front of the aviary. This creates not only a visual barrier, but also a cozy environment where the owner and the parakeets can feel at ease. If a wall serves as part of the demarcation for the aviary, you should install some hooks for toys and perching branches so that the females, who like to gnaw, cannot damage the wall. A thin metal or plexiglass sheet mounted on the wall will prevent your parakeets from damaging your home and, possibly, injuring themselves.

FOR GNAWING AND PERCHING: BRANCHES

Apple
Malus domestica

VEGETATION: A wide-spreading deciduous tree up to 35 feet (10.6 m) high, with gray-brown, scaly bark. **LEAVES:** Green to yellowish-green, underside sometimes with fine hairs, up to 4¼ inches (11 cm) long and 3 inches (7.5 cm) wide, elliptical to egg-shaped, serrate margin. **SPECIAL FEATURES:** Horticultural crop plant with edible, delicious fruits. The large white-to-pink clusters of blossoms are edible for parakeets. Parakeets

also like to gnaw the blossom and leaf buds that appear early in the spring.

White Birch
Betula pendula

VEGETATION: Slender, overhanging, deciduous tree up to 93 feet (28 m) high with white peeling bark that becomes brown and cracked with age. **LEAVES:** Dark green, diamond-shaped to triangular, 2½ inches long by 1½ inches (6 × 4 cm) wide, long-stemmed, shiny top, margin coarsely doubly serrate. **SPECIAL FEATURES:** The catkins are a treat for parakeets. They usually gnaw the leaves at the stem attachment. The soft twigs are great for gnawing and perching.

CRACK WILLOW
Salix fragilis

VEGETATION: Up to 46 feet (14 m) high, broad, spreading to overhanging deciduous tree or bush with gray warty or cracked bark. **LEAVES:** Leaves up to 7 inches (18 cm) long, oblong and pointed, finely serrate margin, leaf stem $3/8$ inch to $3/4$ inch (1–2 cm) long, young leaves finely haired. **SPECIAL FEATURES:** Parakeets are very fond of the yellow catkins that appear at the end of winter as well as the leaves and aromatic wood. The buds that form in the early spring are also a favorite.

Common Hazel
Corylus avellana

VEGETATION: Up to 16 feet (5 m) high deciduous bush. The gray bark is generally smooth but sometimes corklike. **LEAVES:** Initially light green; later dark green, broad, and egg-shaped, up to 6 inches (15 cm) long and 4 inches (10 cm) wide, with hairs on the veins underneath, margin coarsely double serrate. **SPECIAL FEATURES:** The nuts are an insignificant source of parakeet food. The very supple branches and the soft wood are, however, perfect perches and stems for gnawing. The birds like to bathe in wet hazel leaves.

Corkscrew Willow
Salix matsudana (Tortuosa)

VEGETATION: Up to 37 feet (12 m) high, broad, overhanging deciduous tree or bush with branches that twist and turn arbitrarily. The gray-brown bark is thin. **LEAVES:** Narrow light green leaves up to 4 inches (10 cm) long and almost 1 inch (2.5 cm) wide. **SPECIAL FEATURES:** Branches of this willow are often sold in flower shops as decorations. In a glass of water, they are quick to sprout roots and then can be planted in the yard so that fresh twigs are always available. Parakeets love to use the soft, aromatic wood with its fine leaves for perching, climbing, and gnawing. The juicy catkins are a real treat for the birds.

Wild Cherry
Prunus avium

VEGETATION: Broad, column-shaped deciduous tree up to 77 feet (23 m) high, with shiny, red-brown bark that can be removed in rings from the trunk. **LEAVES:** Initially reddish-bronze; later flat, green, hairless, elongated to elliptical, up to 6 inches (15 cm) long and 2½ inches (6 cm) wide, serrate margin, long-stemmed. **SPECIAL FEATURES:** The round fruits are edible when ripe, but the pits, which contain poison-

ous substances, must not be cracked open by the parakeets. The sturdy branches offer excellent perching opportunities, though cherry wood is potentially poisonous to parakeets.

Clever minds always need new ideas for home design.

Swinging and balancing act: coils of rope are almost like natural branches—they are good for the feet and provide a sense of balance.

Luxury Interior Decorating

In domestic bird ownership, aviaries and cages are the private sphere of our feathered family members. This is where they must feel secure and sheltered. The "bird room" must also be set up in such a way that it becomes an appropriate habitat for the birds, which stimulates the parakeets' minds and meets their need to play to their hearts' content and get plenty of exercise. The greater the variety inside the cage or aviary, the better the chances of success.

Parakeets satisfy their tactile sense—the feeling of surfaces—especially through the sensitive soles of their feet and their beaks. In their natural habitat, parakeets experience these sensory impressions when they land on branches, twigs, grasses, stones, and soils of different textures and investigate them with their beaks. In order to provide the birds adequate sensory input in their indoor life, provide them with perches made from different materials. You should also be sure that the birds can wear down their nails, which grow as long as they live. In addition to soft perches, you should also provide perches with a hard, rough surface.

- Good choices are natural perches of various diameters (see pages 16–17). In addition to very thick branches that will accommodate the parakeet's entire foot, you should provide very thin twigs that bend under the bird's weight when it flies onto them. This develops a sense of balance and provides fun in swinging.

- Sand perches are likewise very hard and wear down a parakeet's nails effectively. They are not good choices for permanent perches, however, for they can wear the sensitive soles over time. Put these perches in the cage or aviary so that the parakeets can use them but not stay on them for a long time.

- Softer perches, such as sisal and cotton ropes, are bonuses for aviaries and cages. They are wonderfully flexible and offer many possibilities.

- In setting up the perches, avoid placing them directly above one another. A parakeet's droppings would soil the perch directly beneath.

Toys in the Proper Place

Toys for parakeets are designed either to be mounted directly on the cage or aviary wire or to hang down. Because parakeets usually use small, light toys that often have only a short mounting bracket, they are attached to the roof of the cage. But this means that only the upper part of the aviary or cage is used by the birds, and the lower third is so uninteresting that the birds don't even use it.

You can solve this problem easily with long plastic chains with large links: toys are put in the cage at a variety of heights and levels so it is easy for the parakeets to play with them. Generally, toys are installed so that they hang beside the parakeets and not below the perch.

It is all right if the little fellows have to climb or fly around a toy—that provides exercise and kindles interest in the toy.

The birds usually like swings, coils, and triangles when they are hung very high, so install these toys and perches in the upper part of the aviary.

Tip

Large aviaries provide variety. Small clusters of fairly large stones on the cage floor, on which the parakeets can climb around and in the cracks of which they can search for food, are particularly stimulating. This is a great way for the birds to wear down their nails. Occasionally clean off the stones with a rough sponge.

Climbing Fun for Couch Potatoes

In the wild, parakeets travel great distances to search for food. This life is not only very risky, but it also requires lots of energy. Whenever the little parakeets find something to eat, they have to take in as much as possible. Excess nutrients are stored in adipose tissue. Even though parakeets have now been domesticated for over 200 years, they have not lost this predisposition to store fat reserves. Whereas parakeets in the wild quickly burn off their stored fat, pet birds do not, and many are overweight. Measurements have shown that our parakeets spend 94 percent of each day perched on a branch, rather than tumbling through the air, and this lifestyle often turns them into little slackers that end up getting sick.

In order to keep your pet healthy in the long run, you should set up the interior furnishings of the cage or aviary so that they motivate the birds to walk, hop, climb, and fly as frequently as possible. You can use the following tricks to get the little couch potatoes up to speed:

- Install lots of dead-end branches and perches inside the cage or aviary—that way the parakeets cannot simply walk from one side of the aviary to the other, but rather must climb, hop, or even fly. And flying uses eleven to twenty times more energy than sitting on a branch.

- Always put in branches and perches tipped at an angle. It is much more demanding for the birds to walk up a branch on an incline than to walk along a level one.

- Modify the arrangement of the perches from time to time. Make sure that you don't always position the branches at the same height and angle. The more frequently you alter the setup of the little parakeet room, the more fit your parakeets will be.

- Regularly change the position of the feeding stations. Even set the food dishes alternately very high and low in the aviary; that way you encourage the parakeets to search for food. The water should always be provided far away from the food.

Fitness through variety: continually changing the arrangement of branches and perches keeps your parakeet's mind and body fit.

Construction Manual

For Perching, Climbing, and Swinging: The Atom Ball

Swinging and frolicking is great fun for parakeets. With an atom ball, a combination swing and climbing perch, parakeets can satisfy their need for exercise. This mini outdoor perch is very easy to make, even for beginning hobbyists, and it provides lots of enjoyment for all parakeets.

FOR THE ATOM BALL YOU NEED:

2 polyethylene hoses (from a gardening center), length depending on the desired ball size, outer diameter 1½ inches (4 cm), inner diameter ¾ inch (2 cm); 3 four-way couplings, 4 T couplings; 4 balls of sisal string for wrapping; scissors; 1 plastic chain (any appropriate length); and 1 stainless steel carabiner hook

---

For each half of the ball, make a circle of the desired size with a polyethylene hose and cut it into four equal pieces. Cut four pieces of hose for the inner part a bit longer than the radius of the ball so that you can fit them more precisely later when you assemble the upper and lower parts. The atom ball should not be too large, so that it can swing back and forth a little when a bird lands on it. Connect four long pieces of hose with a four-way coupling (photo 1).

Then use four T-couplings to put together the two halves of the atom ball. Connect the four short sections of hose with a four-way coupling and insert the inner part into the atom ball (photo 2).

Wrap the sisal twine as tightly as possible around the hoses (photo 3). No plastic should be visible so the parakeets cannot gnaw on it. Cut off a link from the plastic chain, thread it through the ball, and mount the open link (see photo, page 24). Attach the carabiner to the chain and hang up the ball.

Tip: The ball is even more stimulating when you weave some colored beads and pieces of wood in with the sisal.

Construction Manual

For Shredding: Rings Made from Paper Plates

Safe, interesting toys for parakeets can be made very simply from very common items. This ring, made from paper plates, is a great pastime for parakeets and is easy to make. The females in particular take advantage of such shredding toys, for they have a greater urge to gnaw than their male counterparts.

FOR THE RING MADE FROM PAPER PLATES YOU NEED:

At least 20 paper plates; 12–16 inches (30–40 cm) of thin steel wire or strong string; 1 plastic chain with large links (any appropriate length); 1 stainless steel carabiner hook; scissors; and as desired: colored beads, thin pieces of wood, untreated pieces of leather, little wicker balls

---

Cut the paper plates into quarters or eighths. Make a hole in the center of every quarter or eighth and string the parts onto a stainless steel wire or the string (photo 1).

Use as many paper plates as it takes to cram them together as tightly as possible—that way the parakeets can gnaw apart the paper better, for their beaks can find many places to attack. If you want to make the ring a little more interesting, string some wooden beads, little wicker balls, thin pieces of wood, or untreated leather between the pieces of paper. If the wooden beads don't have a hole, you will have to drill a tiny one; otherwise the beads will break as they are being drilled.

Bend the wire with the pieces of paper into a ring and thread the two ends of the wire through the last link on the plastic chain. Bend both ends and wind them around tightly so that no sharp end sticks out that could injure the parakeet (photo 2).

The length of the chain is adjusted to suit the size of the cage or aviary. Attach the stainless steel carabiner to the chain and secure the ring in the corner of the cage (photo 3).

Construction Manual

An All-Around Toy: The Wiffle Ball

The Wiffle ball is an all-around favorite among parakeet toys. It is very light and bright, and it has numerous little holes. Wiffle balls are good choices for table games, but they also can be made into other more demanding toys. There are no limits to your imagination.

FOR THE WIFFLE BALL YOU WILL NEED:

1 or more Wiffle balls from a pet shop; 1 fairly long untreated leather thong or sturdy twine; sisal string or bast fiber; tape; colored wood beads of various sizes and shapes; and 1 stainless steel carabiner for a hanger

Bend the leather thong or twine into a loop and hold it together with a little tape. Thread the stub end of the loop through the Wiffle ball and out the other side. Knot the loose ends under the Wiffle ball. Remove the tape from the loop and make a knot (photo 1). The stainless steel carabiner will clip into this for hanging up the Wiffle ball.

Now pull some lengths of sisal string or bast fiber through the holes in the Wiffle ball and thread various beads onto the ends that stick out (photo 2). Depending on your desire and mood, you can thread on a single bead or a whole row of them. Every row of beads is finished off with a good knot at the end (photo 3). Make sure that opposing chains are of about the same length and weight so that the Wiffle ball hangs straight without wobbling too much.

Tip: Several Wiffle balls suspended in a chain serve both as toys and as a climbing apparatus.

Overview: The Perfect Setup

The aviary is the parakeets' playroom; they should feel as comfortable as possible in their home, so don't economize on the furnishings. The aviary should provide just as much optical and acoustic stimulation as it does physical comforts for the birds. The space will be used most effectively if you provide a variety of different perches. The birds will lack nothing, and their daily life will remain interesting.

The atom ball is both a landing spot and a swing. This is a good place to sit with friends, and the parakeets can observe their surroundings at leisure. The sisal twine gives the birds' sensitive feet a gentle massage.

A bundle of twigs and straw is great for pulling apart and shredding.

Left: An assortment of thick twigs with the leaves still on make healthful perches and are great for gnawing.

Right: Spirals like this are a perfect perch for parakeets. Since they swing, the birds automatically get training for their sense of balance. Even little couch potatoes have to exert a bit of effort when they walk up and down the spiral.

Left: Parakeets like ladders made from pieces of natural branch. They can climb to their heart's content and frolic with other members of the flock. The branches are also good for their feet.

Above: Java wood perches are a good alternative to conventional branches in the winter. They are easy to clean, they cannot be destroyed by gnawing, and their irregular thickness enables your parakeet to perform foot gymnastics. The Wiffle ball is also a popular toy.

Above: Climbing nets made from sisal are a challenge for parakeets; where is a body supposed to sit?

Above: Flexible perches such as a rope perch and wood combinations are a real asset, because they make use of open spaces in the aviary.

25

Keeping Parakeets Busy

Our little parakeets need an environment with lots of variety. Appropriate toys and little tasks throughout the day allow the birds to keep measuring themselves against some new challenge.

The parakeet's beak works like tweezers.

Parakeets like to search for their food on the floor and will find even the tiniest seed in the sand.

Food Search Adventure

The ancestors of today's pet parakeets had to survive in a very dry, desolate environment. The wild counterparts of our parakeets still live in desert conditions. In these regions, droughts lasting several years are common. Plus, in the rainy seasons, the parakeets must brave very powerful storms. This extreme environment has turned parakeets into tough survivalists—that is the only way they have a chance to reproduce in nature

and ensure the survival of their species. Still, they live to be only three or four years old in the wild, whereas with good care, pet parakeets can live up to fifteen years. In the open, parakeets can see falling rain at a distance of almost 50 miles (80 km). They have to be able to fly this distance, for they may be able to find something to eat there, thanks to the rain. Since the temperatures in the Australian outback can climb to 104°F (40°C)

Tip

Since male parakeets feed the females extra food, the latter become chubby more quickly. Encourage the females in particular to search for their food. If a female becomes too fat, put it into a **separate cage** in the aviary for a couple of days—that way it maintains contact with the flock but can go on a diet for a while.

during the day, parakeets prefer to search for their food in the early morning and late afternoon. At midday, the parakeets snooze in the leaf canopy of eucalyptus trees, where they are well camouflaged among the foliage.

Parakeets Like a Siesta

This daily rhythm has survived in our pet birds, and you have probably noticed that your parakeets take a long break at midday to rest. But in the morning and the late afternoon, these spirited birds get busy searching for food.

If you give your birds their food only in a dish, this search ends quite quickly. Not only is this unsatisfying for the little parakeets, for they don't experience the feelings associated with the search, but in the long run it is also unhealthy, for the food is easy to get to and they eat too much. Moreover, since parakeets store adipose tissue, they

quickly become overweight and can become seriously ill. Ensure that your parakeet gets the proper amount of food to achieve optimal health.

Food Search: Antidote to Boredom

Parakeets are curious and take an interest in their surroundings. They are always on the lookout for new ways to play, and they fly through their environment on the hunt for food. Scientists call this seeking; it is very satisfying for the birds. If the birds cannot engage in *seeking*, they become bored, listless, and fixated on objects or activities that offer them only vicarious satisfaction. After a while, they often display serious behavior problems.

How do I get into this? Toys filled with treats satisfy the parakeets' need to work for their food.

Work First, Then Food: Foraging

In the wild, parakeets must not only fly very far for their food, but sometimes they also must earn it by climbing and digging. In the process, the birds have to work hard, for they must hold tight to stalks or comb through the dirt for grass seeds. This hard labor to obtain food is known as *foraging*. Studies have shown that birds in captivity prefer to work for their food rather than get it from a dish. If they are given a choice between getting their food in a bowl or obtaining food by solving a problem or performing work in the form of gnawing, digging, or similar tasks, they choose the more demanding route. The prospect of getting an especially tasty reward for strenuous work is fun for the little parakeets, and it keeps them busy during phases of activity.

Foraging, however, is not inborn in parakeets; rather, they must acquire this behavior gradually through a learning process. In the wild, young birds observe how their colleagues search for food in the grass, and they learn from them where food can be found.

Of course, in keeping birds at home, we have to go a different route. In order to satisfy our parakeet's need for seeking and foraging, there are numerous other possibilities in the form of foraging or treat toys.

Starting off Easy

It is important to avoid overtaxing the birds when initially utilizing foraging toys. There is a wide assortment of toys, so make sure you choose an appropriate model that initially presents the birds with an easy challenge—that way they experience success as quickly as possible and have fun doing this type of food search.

Simple foraging toys enable birds to see the food they have to work for and reach (see page 32). At the very beginning of the training, fill this type of toy while the parakeet watches. At first, it is also helpful for the parakeet to sit comfortably on a perch while performing the task. As time goes by, you can remove this comfortable perch and replace it with a more difficult climbing arrangement, for ultimately the birds should have to move in order to reach their food. Foraging toys that hang are installed so that the parakeets have to walk around them— that way they deal with the toy as part of their daily routine.

> ## Tip
>
> For three weeks weigh the amount of food given in the morning and evening and write down the difference. This allows you to come up with the average amount that your parakeets eat in a day. Provide a third of this amount in foraging toys once the parakeets learn how to use them.

Top left: A dish with bird sand and seeds is the simplest form of foraging toy, and it corresponds to parakeets' natural food intake.

Top right: Another simple one: Parakeets quickly figure out a foraging toy with a push-button device.

Left: Only an experienced player can manage to open the lid to this free-swinging toy.

Foraging toys should offer variety, as even parakeets have different preferences. Whereas one parakeet may like lever mechanisms, another may prefer to gnaw to get to its food. Observe your little flock and provide all the possibilities for foraging that your birds like to use.

Once the parakeets get used to this new feeding variant, slowly increase the level of difficulty. Provide a variety of toys and keep changing the location of the toys, to keep the parakeets from getting to their food too quickly.

Important: Control the amount of food provided in order to prevent your parakeet from becoming overweight. It will help if you only provide treats such as millet in the foraging toy or during training.

Construction Manual

Food Toy Made from Paper Plates

If your parakeets don't yet have experience with foraging toys, you can begin with this model made from paper plates. It will ensure that your parakeets will have some variety and a little challenge in their search for food; because the toy is so simple, they will quickly be rewarded with a successful experience.

YOU WILL NEED THE FOLLOWING FOR THE PLATE TOY:

2 common paper plates of the same size (as used for parties and cookouts); 1 thin piece of string (sisal or bast); scissors; and cooked food (from a pet shop: a mix of vegetables, grains, legumes, and millet) or treats that are especially appealing to parakeets

Place the paper plates on top of one another, as pictured, to create a hollow space in the middle. Now cut out four holes arranged in opposing pairs in the edge of the top plate. Cut a fairly large hole in the center of the upper plate and poke holes in the areas between the openings (photo 1). Now tie the plates together by passing the string through the superimposed holes. Don't leave any long ends, and tie the knots very tightly so that the parakeets don't get their nails caught. Fill the space between the plates with lukewarm cooked food (be sure to test the temperature first!) or other treats (photo 2). The parakeets can see the food through the holes. If your birds are slightly more experienced in searching for food, make the holes smaller or leave them out altogether.

Place the toy on the floor of the aviary (photo 3). Be sure that it is not right below a perch, otherwise droppings will land on it. Toys with cooked food must be removed after four hours, for the food spoils quickly. Dry food such as millet can be left in the toy for a longer period of time.

For Nibbling and Swinging: A Muffin Cup Tree

Muffin cups are a great foundation for a foraging toy. Since the papers are heat-resistant, you can use them to serve not only seed treats, but also homemade biscuits. You can find baking mixes in pet shops (bird bread). With their variety of colors, the papers are also a good visual stimulus for the parakeets.

WHAT YOU NEED FOR THE MUFFIN CUP TREE:
Several muffin papers in various colors; 1 long, sturdy length of string or a long leather thong (alternatively, 1 stainless steel fruit skewer for parakeets); colored wood beads or a small wicker ball; 1 stainless steel carabiner; and treats (small pieces of millet, seed balls, etc.)

Select four or five muffin cups, according to how long you want the muffin cup tree to be. Make a small hole in the bottom of each cup. If you want to bake bird muffins yourself, first bake them in the cups and then make a hole through the biscuit and the cup. Thread one or two wooden beads onto the string or the leather thong and make a knot in the end. Now thread a muffin cup on and make another knot in the string so that the cup stays in place (photo 1).

Then string on a couple of wooden beads. Now comes another muffin cup, followed by wood beads (photo 2). Repeat this until the muffin cup tree reaches the desired length. Alternatively, you can string the cups onto a stainless steel fruit skewer.

Fill the cups with treats such as millet and little seed balls. Place shreds of paper on top (photo 3). For experienced parakeets, you can place a paper lid on the cups. Knot the string in a loop, clip on the carabiner, and hang the muffin cup tree inside the cage.

Overview: An Exciting Food Search

Foraging—searching and working hard for food—is part of the life of happy parakeets. For inexperienced birds, simple dishes or muffin cups are adequate. For more experienced parakeets, complicated mechanisms that they have to outsmart are best, and gifted birds can seize a coveted treat from a food toy while swinging back and forth. The main idea is to always provide a new challenge.

Above: Various creations made from tubes and little foam rubber plates (natural rubber) can be made quickly and cheaply. If the little parakeet can't get the millet out of the tube, it can also rip it apart. In either case, it has lots of fun!

Above: In this game, the parakeet must first push a garland made of separate pieces out of the way when it wants to get its treat.

Left: It wiggles and has a cover! Is this little parakeet clever enough to snatch the millet?

Right: A foraging toy for birds in a hurry! Fill ice cube trays with treats, wrap them in a paper towel, and tie them with string. The parakeets first must tear apart the paper towel to get to the seed food in the individual sections, which keeps them busy for quite a while.

Above: This is not only colorful, but also delicious! Muffin cups containing either a homemade bird muffin or seeds and shreds of paper are a very decorative way to present food.

Left: This toy, with openings of various sizes, is a good one for parakeets that like to solve problems. This also involves especially appealing treats.

Above: Healthy nibbles on a wooden skewer. The high point: At the end, even the skewer gets chewed to pieces.

Above: You can put seeds or pieces of millet in the hollows of an origami form. If only it didn't wiggle so much!

Test WHAT KIND OF PLAY DOES YOUR PARAKEET PREFER?

Parakeets have a great variety of personalities and preferences. The spectrum extends from lively go-getters to cautious ditherers. Take this test to find out what kind of play your parakeet prefers. Jot down the letters from the statements that accurately describe your bird.

1 You have set up some **new branches** with leaves inside the cage. Your parakeet immediately climbs on them and **explores them curiously.**   B

2 You have hung up a **new toy.** Your parakeet **sits nervously** in the cage and stretches its neck. Its body language shows that it wants to flee.   A

3 Your parakeet immediately **investigates** and gnaws on **new objects.**   C

4 Colorful, **shiny toys** immediately draw your parakeet's attention, and it plays intensively with these kinds of toys.   B

No pain, no gain: Little slackers must exert some effort to get the reward.

5 Your parakeet never misses a chance to chew up and gnaw paper and cardboard—even the wallpaper.   C

6 If you **change the setup in the cage,** your parakeet refuses to go in it. You can't coax it back in, even with treats.   A

7 Your parakeet keeps itself busy with a toy for a very long time. It is **not distracted,** even by other parakeets.   D

Carefully and always ready for flight, this parakeet investigates whether the toy is truly harmless.

A case for go-getters: It is fun to swing back and forth and check out the colorful beads and pieces of wood.

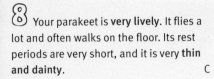 **8** Your parakeet is **very lively**. It flies a lot and often walks on the floor. Its rest periods are very short, and it is very **thin and dainty.**   C

9 Your parakeet eats a lot and **doesn't fly much**. It prefers to sit on its perch and chatter away.   D

10 Your parakeet likes to play with **leather and wood**. It especially likes knots and very thin pieces of wood.   C

How often did you write down A, B, C, or D? Under the letters, read what kind of play your parakeet prefers. If two letters often come up, check under both of them, for it is possible for a parakeet to have mixes of two character types.

KEY

A   Your parakeet is very careful. It feels threatened by new objects and situations. Identify the characteristics of a toy that your parakeet prefers. Choose new toys using these criteria. Give your bird an opportunity to first become familiar with new objects outside the cage.

B   This parakeet type is a go-getter. It can concentrate for only a short time and prefers toys on which it can swing and do gymnastics. This little athlete likes climbing nets, spirals, and hanging ropes, and these items satisfy its need for exercise. Offer it treats in such a way that the little gymnast must fly or climb in order to reach them.

C   Gnawing and chewing things apart are the greatest joy for this type of parakeet. Provide this bird with lots of paper and thin pieces of wood, and replace the destroyed material right away. Wrap up treats in cardboard boxes and paper toys—that way your little chewer always experiences success.

D   Your parakeet is a little slacker, but it can spend a lot more time with a toy. When something interests it, there is scarcely anything that can distract it. Encourage it to exercise with swings and natural twigs, and provide treats only in a foraging toy.

Team-player parakeets: Free flight is fun together.

Come play with me! This parakeet invites its friend to join it in exploring the surroundings.

The High Point of the Day: Free Flight

As extreme athletes, parakeets love free flight. They can let off steam to their heart's content.

The best time for free flight is early morning and late afternoon; that is when the birds are lively and adventurous. On the other hand, midday is not a good choice, for that is when the birds usually take a nap, and they can hardly be motivated to fly.

Ideally, the indoor flight should last at least an hour. Of course, you need to keep an eye on your little flock. On the weekend, when you have more time, the birds can have more time for supervised free flight.

Successful Free Flight

The center of the free flight is a well-designed perch (see pages 40–45). It serves as a landing spot where parakeets can feel secure. Set the perch up with an abundance of toys—that way it becomes a diversified adventure playground that the parakeets will gladly turn to after their flight maneuvers.

In order to prevent unpleasant surprises, you should observe a few rules:

- Stick with the usual safety measures: remove sources of danger, such as poisonous house plants, open doors and windows, and exposed electrical wires.
- Let all family members know when the birds are out on free flight, for parakeets like to walk on the floor. Make sure that no parakeet gets injured from someone stepping on it.
- If you have a mixed flock, you need to make sure that the females do not creep into dark corners and crevices. Even males like to show the females potential nesting sites, which quickly turns free flight into a search for nesting places. Of course, the clever birds will not want to return to their aviary once they find a nesting hole, so avoid the problem by closing off dark areas before free flight.

Stress-Free Return to the Cage

For parakeets, free flight is the high point of the day. It is understandable that they don't always feel like going back into the cage. In this case, make sure that the return is as hassle-free as possible. Here are some helpful tricks:

- Don't fill the food dishes until after free flight. During free flight, offer the birds treats only if you are training the birds. In the meantime, you can give them green food and vegetables, because they don't really make the birds feel full.
- Romping around builds an appetite; a little seed food convinces even stubborn birds

Tip

If a parakeet consistently refuses to go back into the cage, leave it alone in the room. Close the aviary, shut off the lights, and put out some water for the bird. After a while, a hungry parakeet will be waiting for you and will go back into the cage without trouble.

that it is time for a snack in the aviary. If you feed your parakeets processed food, it is even easier; the birds cannot acquire this food on their own, so they find this treat irresistible (see pages 48–49).

Giving your parakeet lots of time for free flight prevents stress in case the parakeet doesn't want to go back in the cage right away.

Construction Manual

Making a Luxury Perch

A perch that quickly turns into a favorite meeting place and landing spot during free flight is quite easy to build with a little manual skill. The necessary materials can be found in any building supplies store. The perch consists of a simple solid basic frame that can be accessorized with a series of new toys. This turns the perch into a diversified habitat that is always interesting to the parakeets.

TOOLS
- ☐ Hand saw
- ☐ Cordless drill
- ☐ Drill press, if available
- ☐ High-speed drills, 3/32 inch, 1/4 inch, 5/32 inch, 3/16 inch, 5/16 inch (2.5 mm, 4 mm, 5 mm, 6 mm, 8 mm), for countersinking
- ☐ Wood drills, 3/8 inch, 15/32 inch, 5/8 inch, 25/32 inch (10 mm, 12 mm, 16 mm, 20 mm)
- ☐ 2 small clamps
- ☐ Large screwdriver
- ☐ 120-grit sandpaper for rounding edges
- ☐ Pencil and ruler

MATERIALS
For the base plate:
- ☐ 1 sheet of plywood, 20 inch × 20 inch × 3/4 inch (50 × 50 × 2 cm), laminated and waterproof
- ☐ 2 strips of wood, 20 inch × 1 1/4 inch × 1/4 inch (50 × 3 × 0.5 cm), hardwood
- ☐ 2 strips of wood, 20 inch × 1 1/4 inch × 1/4 inch (50 × 3 × 0.5 cm), hardwood
- ☐ 12 wood screws, 5/32 inch × 1 inch (4 × 25 mm)
- ☐ 4 steel drywall screws, 9/16 inch × 2 3/4 inch (14 × 70 mm)

For the stands:
- ☐ Piece of wood (spruce or hardwood), 2 inch × 2 inch × 5 feet (5 × 5 × 152 cm)
- ☐ 3 screw-in lugs, 1/4 inch × 1 1/2 inch (6 × 40 mm)
- ☐ 3 steel countersink screws, 1/4 inch × 1 1/2 inch (6 × 40 mm)
- ☐ 2 pieces of plywood, 4 1/2 inch × 2 inch × 3/8 inch (11 × 5 × 1 cm)
- ☐ 2 strips of plywood, 2 inch × 3/4 inch × 3/8 inch (5 × 2 × 1 cm)
- ☐ 2 strips of plywood, 2 inch × 3/8 inch × 1/4 inch (5 × 1 × 0.5 cm)
- ☐ Wood glue (non-toxic)

For the cube:
- ☐ 1 length of beech, 2 inch × 2 inch (5 × 5 cm), cut into 8 cubes, 2 inch (5 cm) each
- ☐ Hardwood dowels each 3 feet (1 m) long
  5 pieces 1/2 inch (12 mm) diameter,
  2 pieces 3/8 inch (10 mm) diameter,
  3 pieces 5/8 inch (16 mm) diameter,
  2 pieces 3/4 inch (20 mm) diameter
- ☐ 2 ceiling hooks, 1/8 inch × 1 1/2 inch (3 × 40 mm) (steel, with wood screw threads)

Note: All dimensions in the instructions apply to the center of the hole.

Mmm! The perch decorated with fresh branches is a welcome addition!

The Base

Mark the center of the plywood and draw a square 2 inches (5 cm) on a side in the center of the wood. Use a $^3/_{16}$ inch (6 mm) bit to drill four holes in the square. The holes must be countersunk from the bottom side. Now use a $^5/_{32}$ inch (5 mm) bit to drill slightly countersunk holes in the plywood strips. Spread some glue on the edges. Screw the 20-inch (50 cm) strips to two opposite sides of the plywood sheet using $^5/_{32}$ inch × 1 inch (5 × 25 mm) screws. The plywood strips project upward. Screw the two 20-inch (50 cm) strips to the two other sides of the wood.

The Stands

The diagram at the right shows the top part of the 2 × 2 upright stand. Mark the locations of the holes on the upright stand. First drill a $^1/_2$ inch (12 mm) hole completely through the stand 2 inches (5 cm) from the top edge. Then on the same side, drill a $^5/_{16}$ inch (8 mm) hole through the stand $10^1/_2$ inches (26.5 cm) from the top edge. Now turn the stand ninety degrees to the right and drill a $^3/_8$ inch (1 cm)

hole, 1 inch (2.5 cm) from the top edge. Then use a $^1/_4$ inch (6 mm) bit to drill $1^1/_4$ inches (3 cm) deeper in the center of the hole. On the same side, drill through the stand 11 inches (27.5 cm) from the top edge, with a $^5/_8$ inch (16 mm) bit. Turn the stand back ninety degrees and use the $^3/_8$ inch (10 mm) bit to drill holes $^3/_8$ inch (1 cm) deep for the clamp mounts $5^1/_2$ inches (14 cm) and 24 inches (60 cm) from the top edge. Drill both $^3/_8$ inch (10 mm) holes $1^1/_4$ inches (3 cm) deeper with a $^1/_4$ inch (6 mm) bit. Now carefully screw in the lugs until they are flush or even slightly below the surface. Finally, drill a $^5/_8$ inch (16 mm) hole $1^1/_2$ inches (4 cm) deep in the face of the stand.

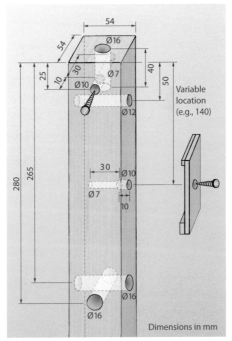

The drilled holes in the upper part of the stand.

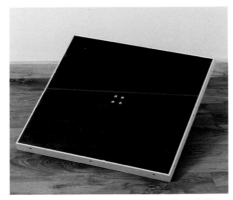

The solid base plate gives the perch stability.

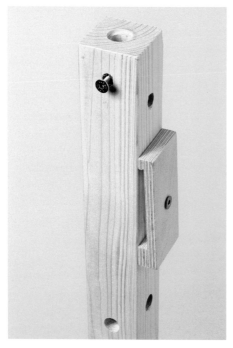

The clamp mounts hold branches for gnawing.

The cube is the basic framework for the perch.

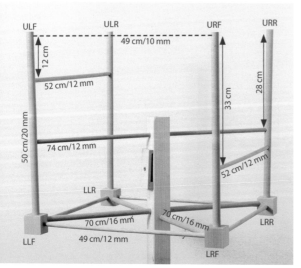

Clamp Mounts: In the center of the two $4^{1}/_{2}$ inch × 2 inches × $^{3}/_{8}$ inch (11 × 5 × 1 cm) pieces of plywood, drill a hole with the $^{1}/_{4}$ inch (6 mm) bit and slightly countersink it. Onto one end of the $4^{1}/_{2}$ inch (11 cm) pieces, glue a piece of plywood $^{1}/_{4}$ inch (6 mm) thick, and a $^{3}/_{8}$ inch (10 mm) piece onto the other end. Clamp the ends in place until they are dry.

The Cube

Corner Cube: Thoroughly sand all the edges of the corner cubes. Sand one edge until it has a bevel $^{5}/_{32}$-inch (4 mm) wide (see photo below). Mark the center of all cubes and drill a $^{3}/_{4}$-inch (20 mm) hole $^{5}/_{8}$ inch (1.5 cm) deep in the top face. Now place four cubes together so that the four bevels point to the center and the drilled hole is on top. Designate the four lower cubes LLR (lower left rear), LRR (lower right rear), ULF (upper left front), and URF (upper right front).

Then place the four upper cubes onto the other ones with the bevels facing toward the center and the drilled holes facing downward, and mark them accordingly (ULR, URR, ULF, URF). Drill the lower blocks $^{3}/_{8}$ inch (1 cm) deep with the $^{1}/_{2}$ inch (12 mm) bit on the right and the left of the bevel. Drill a

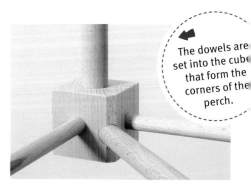

The dowels are set into the cube that form the corners of the perch.

hole $^3/_8$ inch (1 cm) deep in the upper blocks with the $^3/_8$ inch (10 mm) bit. Now drill corresponding holes in the URR and the ULF blocks about $^5/_8$ inch (1.5 cm) deep in the center of the bevel with the $^5/_8$ inch (16 mm) bit. The distance from the lower edge of the block to the center of the hole is $^1/_2$ inch (1 cm). Do the same to the LLR and LRF blocks, but in this case the distance from the bottom edge of the block to the center of the hole is $^3/_4$ inch (2 cm).

Finishing the Dowels: Saw the two $^3/_4$ inch (20 mm) dowels into four pieces 19$^1/_2$-inches (49.5 cm) long. These form the four vertical edges of the cube. Determine the top side of the dowels and mark them with LF (left front), RF (right front), LR (left rear), and RR (right rear). Use the $^1/_2$ inch (12 mm) bit to drill a hole $^3/_8$ inch (1 cm) deep in the RR and RF dowels 13 inches (33 cm) from the top edge. Use the $^1/_2$ inch (12 mm) bit to drill a hole $^3/_8$ inch (1 cm) deep in the LR and LF dowels 4$^3/_4$ inches (12 cm) from the top edge. Drill a hole in the RR and RF dowels offset about 45 degrees from the first hole and 11 inches (27.5 cm) from the upper edge. Then cut two $^1/_2$-inch (12 mm) dowels into four pieces 19$^3/_{16}$ inches (49 cm) long; these form the lower edges of the cube. For the cross braces on the sides, trim two more $^1/_2$ inch (12 mm) dowels to 20$^{11}/_{32}$ inches (52 cm); trim the last $^1/_2$ inch (12 mm) dowel to 28$^{13}/_{16}$ inches (73 cm). Cut two $^3/_8$-inch (10 mm) dowels into four pieces 19$^3/_{16}$ inches (49 cm) long for the top edges of the cube. Then saw three $^5/_8$ inch (16 mm) dowels to a length of 27$^1/_2$ inches (70 cm); these form the lower and upper diagonals. For the

The finished perch.

ceiling hooks, drill a $^3/_{32}$ inch (2.5 mm) hole in the upper diagonal dowel 6 inches (15 cm) from the ends and screw the hooks into place (see photo above).

The Perch Is Done!

Drill four holes in the stands from underneath with the $^3/_{32}$ inch (2.5 mm) bit and screw them tightly to the base plate with drywall screws $^3/_{16}$ inch × 2$^3/_4$ inches (4.5 × 70 mm). Screw on the clamp mounts using $^1/_4$ inch × 1$^1/_2$ inches (6 × 40 mm) screws. Now turn the screw into the uppermost hole on the side. Place the lower diagonal through the vertical member, put a little glue onto the cubes, and insert the upper dowels. Insert the vertical and diagonal dowels, and finally assemble the upper cubes, dowels, and diagonals.

43

Overview: The Perch as a Gathering Spot

A perch presents parakeets with an area to land, and is a place for playing and resting. In addition to freestanding perches, there are space-saving variations for smaller homes, such as models that hang or are built into the cage and fold out easily.

Important: The perch must be placed in such a way that the birds cannot be injured by slamming doors. They must feel secure in their homes.

Above: A well-constructed tabletop perch made from snakeroot branches is economical and can be embellished with new toys. It can be put away quickly and easily after free flight.

Right: Hanging perches fit into the smallest home and still provide space for a fairly large flock of parakeets.

Left: This is fun! Hanging ropes of various thicknesses with knots tied in them are great swings and an interesting landing spot. Cut long, loose fibers off daily with scissors so that lively birds don't get their claws tangled in them.

Right: Homemade perching rings woven from fresh willow branches are an economical play area where the birds can gnaw and swing. If the green perch gets gnawed through, a new ring can be woven quickly from fresh twigs.

Above: Dead-end java wood branches can be mounted on the wall. This provides a climbing wall for older parakeets that motivates them to hop, fly, and climb. On full-length branches, they would simply walk from one side of the cage to the other.

Left: Small but super! Colorful wheel swings quickly become favorite resting spots. They are often coveted to the point that each parakeet demands one for its exclusive use.

Above: Whether homemade or purchased, a triangle with a toy hanging in the center is twice as nice.

Above: Climbing nets are good for protecting large windows. The visual barrier helps the birds put on the brakes on time and land if they don't have enough room.

HEADS UP! WHEN TWO PARAKEETS LIKE EACH OTHER, LEARNING IS TWICE AS MUCH FUN!

The Little School for Parakeets

Parakeets learn throughout their lifetimes. Their quick reaction time and perceptiveness ensure survival in the wild, and make them both teachable and demanding training partners in the home.

Birds that eat their vegetables also deserve an occasional treat.

Vegetables are healthful, keep the birds slender, and call for good table manners—so they are an ideal snack between meals.

Food as a Learning Tool

It is fun to watch parakeets when they play, and to study their social contact. You can have even more fun with your feathered housemates when you are part of the fun. Since parakeets, who are kept in multiples, at first show little interest in contact with the owner, conditions have to be satisfied so that the birds will cooperate. The basis for a training program that both parties will like is the proper feed.

By their nature, parakeets have established feeding times—especially in the morning and afternoon. In between, they rest, play, and enjoy the other members of their flock. You should also imitate this pattern with pet birds; feed your parakeets only at established times, and don't keep food available to them all day long. This gives you a chance to tempt the birds with a treat during training. For high-quality, balanced nutrition, it is recommended to switch the parakeets over to a basic diet of processed food. Processed food (from a pet shop) is a complete food that consists of baked seeds and grains, and contains all the vitally important ingredients for the birds. The advantage is that the parakeets cannot pick through for their favorite grains and get too fat. The birds thus avoid becoming overweight, and treats and grains remain interesting to them as rewards.

Switch over to processed food slowly, for parakeets are conservative. At first, mix one part processed food with three parts grain food. As soon as the birds eat the processed food reliably, the grain food—in small portions—is used only as a treat in the foraging toy or as a reward during training.

Training at the Right Time

Always train and play with your parakeets before mealtimes, when the birds are motivated and happy to get the treats. No bird plays with its belly full; all it wants to do is digest and take a rest. A filled food dish comes only as a reward after training. Always train in very short sequences, for parakeets can concentrate for only short times and are easily distracted. It is better to work with the birds two to three times a day for three to five minutes each time than one time a day for fifteen minutes.

Training for Young and Old: Parakeets of any age can be trained. Parakeets can learn to step onto your hand or to climb a ladder at only a few weeks old. Sometimes senior

Motivation required: A little bit of millet creates interest in the next step in training.

> ## Tip
> Even if you work all day long, you must not forgo training with your parakeets. It doesn't matter if you occasionally have no time for practice—the parakeets don't forget what they have learned. It is very important that you give them processed food, millet, and grains only during training.

parakeets need a little longer if you have not yet worked with them. Since parakeets learn throughout their lifetimes, however, there is no reason not to train even senior birds. Sometimes old birds can even concentrate significantly better than adolescent parakeets.

FEATURE: WHICH TREATS ARE HEALTHFUL?

Foxtail Millet

Hardly any parakeet can resist this treat. Foxtail millet is useful both as a reward during training and as a nutritional diet if a parakeet ever gets sick. The millet kernels are about $^5/_{64}$ inches (2 mm) in size, and they have a high content of easily digested carbohydrates—that is why they can make birds fat if they are fed too much. Store the treats in a plastic container in the refrigerator and feed the little kernels individually. If you want to offer your flock of parakeets a whole cluster of millet once a week, set it up in such a way that the parakeets have to fly and climb to get the grain.

Bird Muffins

Bird muffins are baked using special baking mixtures for birds. They are even healthier when you grate carrot, kohlrabi, or zucchini into the dough. The parakeets can gnaw through the paper forms. Offer the muffins in a muffin cup tree so that the birds have to expend some effort to get at the treats (see page 33). Freeze excess muffins. If you let the muffins dry out, they become hard and are fun to gnaw.

Chew Sticks

Chew sticks and seed balls are to parakeets as chocolate is to humans. They come in a wide variety of flavors. Their sugar and fat content is often very high, however, so they can make your parakeet overweight if they are eaten too frequently. Seed balls are great for hiding in treat toys, for they are small and easy to dispense. You should offer your birds chew sticks a maximum of once a week. Set them up in the cage so that it is difficult for the parakeets to reach them.

Bird Bread

Leftover bread is very appealing to parakeets; however, our bread is not suitable as a treat for parakeets. A better choice is special bird bread baking mixes that contain no salt or additives that could harm the birds. Pet shops sell various flavors, so you can offer your parakeets their favorite variety. Of course, you should also add herbs and grated vegetables to the baking mix to make them more nutritious. Store the slices of bread in a plastic container in the freezer and thaw them before serving.

Fresh Herbs

Herbs such as basil, parsley, and sorrel are a healthy, tasty alternative to treats that contain fat and sugar. You can also offer these treats during free flight. Because they are great for tearing apart, they are also a fine way to keep the parakeets busy. In the winter, you can also put pots of herbs into the cage as a treat for your parakeets. Many parakeets even like to use moist herbs as a bathing place!

Grain Food

Grain food is not only a basic food for parakeets, but it is also a treat that is high in calories. Depending on the manufacturer, mixes available on the market contain a greater or lesser quantity of millet. But because parakeets have a tendency to become overweight, you should control the portions of this food. Parakeets that know grain food exclusively as a treat and a reward are easily lured with a few grains. This is why

it is ideal for luring recalcitrant birds back into the aviary after free flight. Grain food should be stored in a plastic container in the refrigerator.

If this little parakeet learns early, it can turn into a skilled puzzle solver!

Tricky tasks like this can be performed only by graduates of parakeet elementary school.

A Little Educational Theory

Like most animals, parakeets learn in two ways. On the one hand, they are curious and want to investigate unfamiliar things; on the other, they are quick to notice that they get a reward for a specific behavior. The type of reward that an bird deems worthy of striving for can vary greatly. Whereas the owner's attention is very important to one parakeet, with others nothing gets done without a treat. And for very timid parakeets, too much attention can even be a strain.

Learning with Positive Reinforcement

The more interesting and desirable the reward for a specific behavior is, the more often the animal will display this behavior on its own. It makes no difference what kind of behavior is involved. The only important

Tip

Quite often people don't even realize that they have reinforced a parakeet's behavior negatively. Observe yourself closely as you deal with the birds. Take note of situations in which you have unconsciously used negative reinforcement, and develop a positive reinforcement to reach the same goal.

thing is that the bird connects the displayed behavior with the subsequent reward and learns that this precise behavior pays off. This learning process is known as positive reinforcement. Parrots and parakeets are among the birds that learn throughout their lifetimes. They retain learned behaviors forever, for a completed learning process cannot be reversed. If a parakeet learns how to climb onto your hand, it will do this when it gets the reward that it wants (positive reinforcement).

AVOIDING NEGATIVE REINFORCEMENT

A parakeet can also form the impression that the owner is forcing it into the cage by hand. When this happens, it flutters around, and when the hand is withdrawn from the cage, the bird learns that fluttering about wildly causes the hand to go away. In this case, the removal of the hand also serves as a reward. This type of process is referred to as negative reinforcement, for the hand was an unpleasant stimulus that was removed when the parakeet fluttered its wings. In this way, the parakeet learns that flapping around leads to the "reward" that it wants.

If you work with negative reinforcement, you will never experience more than minimal success with your bird. The unpleasant stimulus is removed, and the bird no longer has any reason to display the desired behavior. With positive reinforcement, on the other hand, the bird is motivated from within to display a specific behavior, for in exchange it gets the desired reward. You should therefore work only with positive reinforcement in training so that you win the trust of your parakeets and the birds have fun playing with you.

The best qualification for learning is trusting togetherness. From its high perch, the parakeet has everything securely in view.

Clever: Clicker Training

A clicker is one useful aid for training parakeets to perform tricks; it is a small instrument that clicks and can be used to signal acoustically the precise behavior that you want to reinforce. The clicker marks the end of a behavior, and the bird knows that it now gets a treat. It is important to choose a quiet clicker, for loud clicking noises make parakeets feel insecure. First, every parakeet needs to learn what the click noise means. Offer the bird a piece of millet and click on the precise instant when the bird eats the millet. The parakeet must associate the clicking sound with the millet. If a parakeet is still very wary and doesn't approach your hand close enough, first place a piece of millet through the bars into the food dish inside the cage. Remain seated near the cage and watch when the parakeet eats the millet. Press the clicker at that precise instant. Once the bird has eaten the piece of millet, place a new piece of millet into the dish and repeat the process.

Slowly approach the cage so that the bird gets used to having you nearby. Closely observe the parakeet's body language. If the bird displays anxiety, go back to a place in the room where it remains relaxed. Once you have worked your way up to the cage, leave your hand motionless near the food dish so that the parakeet gets used to it. Your hand should lie still at a level lower than the parakeet. As soon as the bird calmly takes the piece of millet from the food dish, place the piece of millet into the dish by reaching in through the cage door. If the parakeet also accepts this without problem, offer pieces of millet from your hand. Don't forget to activate the clicker every time the parakeet eats some millet.

Important: The pieces of millet must be very small so you can reinforce the bird's behavior as often as possible without feeding it too much.

Not for the Timid: The Target Stick

Once the bird has learned the meaning of the clicking sound, introduce the target stick. This involves a small rod that you use to show the bird, for example, in which direction it must move. The target stick is also useful with timid birds, because you can train them from a greater distance.

Target sticks with a built-in clicker that are used for parrots are not appropriate for parakeets. They are too large and frighten the birds.

When the clicker is activated, the parakeet knows that it will soon get a treat. Later on it will do the exercise when it merely hears the noise.

Top left: Once the initial shyness disappears, give the treat by hand. Click at the instant the bird eats.

Top right: Click at the instant the parakeet touches the target stick with its beak.

Below: Now hold the target stick a short distance from the parakeet so that the bird has to walk toward it.

First, let the parakeet touch the end of the rod with its beak and click at that precise instant. Then immediately give it a treat. The bird learns that touching the end of the rod is the behavior that is rewarded. Now slowly move the tip away from the bird so that it must follow it if it wants a treat—that way you can lead the parakeet to a specific location.

Make Learning Fun

Whether you use a clicker, a target stick, or both in your efforts to train your parakeets, you should always keep one point in mind: learning must be fun for the birds, or they won't cooperate with you. If you see that your parakeets are upset, stop the training until the birds calm down.

FOR EXERCISE BUFFS: SKATEBOARDING IS A REAL TEST OF COURAGE.

Tricks for Parakeets

Clever minds need a series of challenges to keep their skills sharp. Regular training is a must, because it increases a parakeet's sense of well being. And it is great fun for both human and bird when a new trick works out.

A parakeet will land on your finger only when it trusts you completely.

The parakeet is totally relaxed as it sits on the hand—this is the first step to a long friendship.

Hand Taming Parakeets

All parakeet owners want their birds to perch on their hands, for daily life and training are much simpler when the birds are hand tame. But this is a major step for the birds; after all, they are prey animals and are instinctively afraid of an animal that is a lot larger than they are. So don't be surprised if you begin with the step-up exercises and your parakeets at first react with anxiety; this is normal. In order to reduce mistrust,

you must never use force when training your birds. Show them respect and patience—this is the best recipe for gradually building up trust between you and your parakeets. During training, always observe the birds' body language and pull back as soon as they show any anxiety. Approach the cage with slow movements and speak to the birds in a calm voice. And don't forget: A little treat usually helps to break the ice!

Instructions

Step-up for Beginners

This step-up exercise is the simplest variant and is appropriate for all parakeets–from casual young birds to cautious ones, and even nervy specimens. The bird is lured with a plate of grains, and the approach to the hand happens almost incidentally.

DIFFICULTY ★ ☆ ☆ ☆ ☆

MATERIALS
Ceramic dish with grain food

Create a calm atmosphere in the room where the parakeets have their free flight. Sit at a table with a book or a newspaper, and place a ceramic dish with grain food on the table a short distance away. Read for a while and don't pay any attention to the dish. Don't even look at it if the parakeet flies to the dish and eats the grains, for the bird will take this direct staring as a threat if it does not yet trust you. When you are done reading, take the dish away. Once this goes well several days in a row, place the dish closer to you so that the parakeet gets used to you being close (photo 1). Always observe its body language and work in small steps. The parakeet must always feel secure. Eventually you can place the dish on your opened hand (photo 2).

Once the bird accepts this and hops onto the dish, you can offer the grain food by hand. Don't move your hand when the parakeet lands on it. Only when this becomes routine can you carefully raise your hand a little (photo 3).

Instructions

Step-up in the Cage

Many owners are afraid that their parakeets won't want to return to the cage after their free flight. If you feel that way, you should first get your birds used to your hand with this step-up variant in the cage. Then there will be no stress outside the cage, and the birds will let you put them back into the cage after their free flight.

DIFFICULTY ★ ★ ☆ ☆ ☆

MATERIALS
Cage with large door, dead-end perch, millet

For this exercise, you need a cage with a large door so you can reach in easily. Install at least one branch or perch in the cage in such a way that it has one free end that sticks out into the center of the cage at a height that is comfortable for you. Use fairly large pieces of millet as a reward at first.

Hold one finger as an extension to the end of the perch. Use the other hand to offer the parakeet a piece of millet in such a way that it must stretch to reach your hand (photo 1). Observe whether the bird is relaxed in the presence of your hand.

As soon as the bird's body language tells you that it wants the treat, slowly move the millet toward the finger that is still calmly placed against the perch. With a little patience, the parakeet will soon place one foot onto your finger (photo 2).

Eventually the parakeet will dare to step completely onto your hand (photo 3). Feed it again and slowly place it onto another perch. Once the bird gets used to this exercise, give it a signal (e.g., "step-up"), which the bird can connect with the act of climbing onto your finger. Whenever this works, praise the bird heartily, but give it only small pieces of millet. Soon it will climb onto your finger even without a treat.

Instructions

Step-up for Reluctant Birds

Many parakeets lose their shyness with their owners, but they don't dare to take the last step up. They keep flying around nervously and get flustered because perhaps they have had a bad experience with hands. You can use this step-up variant to help such birds overcome their anxieties.

DIFFICULTY ★ ★ ☆ ☆ ☆

MATERIALS
Stick the same thickness as the perch (e.g., a wooden spoon), millet

For this exercise, use a stick with the same diameter as the familiar perch as an extension of your hand. A wooden kitchen spoon is a good choice. Because the birds generally have no fear of perches, this aid will work very well. Tie a fairly long piece of millet to the end of the stick and offer it to the parakeet. Hold the stick by the end rather than the middle. Make this feeding part of the daily routine. Then gradually reduce the distance until your hand is right by the millet (photo 1).

As soon as the parakeet calmly takes the millet, proceed to placing the millet right on your hand (photo 2). Because the parakeet gets used to the daily feeding on the stick, with time it will fly to your finger instead of the stick (photo 3).

Do not move at first; otherwise, the bird will become frightened and the slowly developing trust will be destroyed. Enjoy the fact that the bird is with you and speak softly to it. Only when you have the sense that the bird is relaxed can you slowly move with it in the room or place it into the cage.

With a little patience, every timid birds can learn the eagle exercise.

Sports and preventive medicine together: the eagle exercise. Are the feathers under the wings in good shape?

Games and Tricks without Props

Playing and training should be fun for both you and your parakeet. To get your clever bird used to the training, you can begin with exercises that use no props—this is easier for both training partners. Here is one ground rule: Practice only movement sequences and behaviors that correspond to the parakeet's natural behavior. If you concentrate on the bird's body language, you will discover many possibilities—such as lifting the wings in the

eagle exercise or rotating on its own axis in the turn-around. Of course, your feathered students initially don't know what to do. Only when you praise the birds for a certain behavior in a timely fashion and reward them with a treat do they learn which behavior is desired and worth their while. Eventually you can connect every exercise with another verbal command so that it is performed merely on demand.

Game Instructions

Wings up: The Eagle Exercise

With the eagle exercise you can encourage a totally normal behavior from your parakeets—specifically, lifting and extending the wings. This exercise also serves as a tool for checking the underside of the wings, so that you can detect skin or plumage problems sooner. As always, be sure to reinforce the behavior at precisely the right instant.

DIFFICULTY ★ ★ ★ ☆ ☆

MATERIALS
T- or U-stand, treats, possibly the clicker

Call the parakeet onto a T- or a U-stand and reinforce it with a treat for having come to you. Now speak to the little bird and give it attention. As soon as it coincidentally lifts its wings a bit, immediately say "eagle" and give it a piece of millet (photo 1). Do this even if it lifts just one wing (photo 2).

When your parakeet links lifting the wings briefly with the command and the giving of a treat and repeats it regularly, give the bird plenty of praise, but don't give it any more treats.

Only when it lifts the wings a bit higher do you reinforce it with another treat (photo 3). Thus, you now reward only progress in learning, but you praise with your voice every time the exercise is done successfully. Meanwhile, the parakeet understands that raising the wings on command is reinforced.

Keep bringing up this exercise in the daily routine—that way you reinforce it continuously. If you find it difficult to reinforce a quick lift of the wings at the right instant, work with the clicker.

Waiting and Coming When Called

Game Instructions

Even though this exercise appears easy, it is a real challenge for most parakeets. They don't understand the meaning of *waiting*. Wild parakeets don't know this behavior, for it is not necessary in the wild. But with domesticated birds, it is very useful for a parakeet to wait and come when called.

DIFFICULTY ★ ★ ★ ★ ★

MATERIALS
T-stand or perch, treats

Lure your parakeet to a T-stand or perch. Praise it generously and give it confirmation with a very small treat. Now give the bird a hand signal by lifting the index finger (photo 1), and praise the bird again. Once the parakeet gets used to the hand signal, count quietly. At first the bird should remain on the perch only three to five seconds, but you should then lengthen the time up to a minute. Remain standing near the bird during this time. Once the bird waits successfully, take the bird onto your finger, praise it, and give it a treat. In the next step, communicate by means of a raised finger that the little bird must wait, and step away from it a bit so that it must hop or fly when you call it to your finger after the waiting time (photo 2).

Gradually increase the distance between you and the bird. Because the parakeet has learned to wait, it will stay in place until you give it the signal to come (photo 3). If the bird flies too early, do not reward it, and bring it back to its waiting station. Then keep working across a shorter distance, for the bird's learning process is not yet completed.

For the Timid: Turn Around

Turning around on the bird's axis is a fine exercise for birds that are not yet hand tame. This can also be done in the cage with the door open, and it gives the owner and a timid bird an opportunity to have contact with one another without putting any pressure on the bird. This develops a routine and increases trust.

DIFFICULTY ★ ★ ☆ ☆ ☆

MATERIALS
Perch, treats, possibly the clicker

For this exercise, your parakeet should be on a perch that you can reach easily. Coax the parakeet onto the perch with a treat and give it confirmation with praise and a treat. Show the bird a second treat and note whether the bird wants it. It should follow the treat with its eyes (photo 1).

Now move the treat under the perch and to the other side so that the parakeet has to turn around if it wants to get the treat. Move your hand to the front again (photo 2). The parakeet should turn around (photo 3). As soon as the bird perches in front of you again, reward it with a treat. Make sure that the parakeet makes a complete turn. If it makes only a half turn at first and sits with its back to you, give it praise at the rear of the perch. Many parakeets are uneasy when people put their hands under them. Don't move your hand above the bird, but rather around it—thus you move the treat from one hand to the other. Because you need both hands for this, you work without the clicker.

A trick toy is used only in training.

A perfect parakeet toy is a small, light mesh ball, for the little bird can pick it up easily.

Games and Tricks with Props

As soon as your parakeets master various games without props, you can attempt some slightly more complicated tasks—for example, incorporating various toys into the exercises. However, you have to make sure that they are easy for parakeets to handle so that the birds enjoy using them. In addition to the universally liked mesh ball, there are also little plastic cars, swings, ring games, and tubes and tunnels for parakeets.

In order for a learning toy to retain its appeal for the birds, it should be available only during the training sessions and in connection with the trainer; that is the only way that the parakeets understand that it is now playtime. This increases their alertness, for they know that momentarily they will be able to earn an additional treat. Your parakeets' motivation also increases as soon as you get the toy out of the box, and your birds will gladly cooperate.

Up and Down with the Seesaw

It is no great feat for a parakeet to walk along a wobbly branch—that is part of its routine in the wild. But things are different if, for example, the solid ground suddenly begins to move and tip. Normally a parakeet would fly away immediately, but if it continues walking instead, it is among the gifted parakeets!

DIFFICULTY ★ ★ ★ ★ ☆

MATERIALS
A small wooden seesaw (e.g., for pet rodents), target stick, cellophane tape, possibly the clicker, millet

Place the seesaw onto an empty table and lure the parakeet close to the seesaw with a little piece of millet. If the bird is very shy, take the target stick and coax it close to the seesaw with the stick. Reinforce every step that the bird takes in the direction of the seesaw until it reaches the toy (photo 1).

Now lure the parakeet to the center of the seesaw (photo 2). The seesaw must not yet tip—first the parakeet must get over its timidity with the new toy. If necessary, you can tape the low end of the seesaw in place where it contacts the table.

Now comes the hardest part of the exercise: The parakeet must walk the length of the seesaw while it tips. If you have taped the seesaw in advance, remove the tape and use the target stick to coax the bird along the seesaw (photo 3).

If the parakeet flies off when the seesaw tips, help it on the next attempt by holding the seesaw and letting it tip very slowly. Very hesitant birds need constant reinforcement as they walk along the seesaw. In this case, continually give the bird some millet until it feels more confident. Gradually, you can give pieces of millet less frequently.

Game **Instructions** ## Pushing a Toy Car

Pushing a small, light toy car is consistent with the natural movements of parakeets. In the outdoors, these birds also walk on the ground in search of food. Their long legs and their very high running speed, in comparison to their diminutive size, are ideal for integrating this movement into a sports exercise.

DIFFICULTY

★ ★ ★ ☆ ☆

MATERIALS

A small, light plastic toy vehicle, target stick, treats

Pushing a small toy car is child's play for trained parakeets.

A requirement for this exercise is that your parakeet must willingly take food from your hand. Completely clear off the table on which you intend to practice this exercise, and put nothing on the table except the little plastic vehicle. Coax your parakeet onto the table with a little food and hold the target stick. As with clicker training, the parakeet must first learn to touch the tip of the target stick with its beak. If the little bird is skeptical at first, reinforce any approach or movement toward the target stick with ample praise and a treat. As soon as the parakeet reliably bites the tip of the target stick or touches it, begin to lead it around the top of the table with the stick. Your parakeet should follow the target stick everywhere, and every time it touches the stick the bird must be given praise.

Now hold the target stick above the car so that the tip points over the rear and a good portion of it projects beyond. The goal is for the bird to push the vehicle forward. Keep this starting position the same, for otherwise the little bird will become confused. The parakeet will now run to the tip of the target stick and bite it (photo 1).

Give it praise, and slowly and continually pull the target stick closer to the vehicle so that the tip keeps coming closer to the back (photo 2). Eventually the tip of the target stick is even with the car, and the parakeet touches both at the same time with its beak (photo 3). Now give it generous praise, for your parakeet has made it over the first major hurdle.

Full Speed Ahead

As soon as the parakeet understands that it should run to the rear of the car and touch it with its beak, slowly reduce the treats and remove the target stick from the exercise. Encourage the parakeet to touch the car, and as soon as it moves a tiny bit, praise the bird generously and give it a good treat. From now on, give the bird confirmation and praise only when it moves the car a short distance (photo 4). Because the vehicle is very light, this will not be difficult for the parakeet. At first, provide praise every time

the car moves, and then only every other time. Watch your parakeet's body language. If it seems distracted or indifferent and looks around, immediately stop the exercise and have it do a simple exercise without an aid that you can praise immediately. Over time and with continuous practice, the parakeet will push the car all around the table.

Photo 3: Praise effusively when the bird touches both the stick and the car.

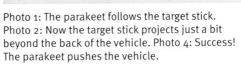

Photo 1: The parakeet follows the target stick. Photo 2: Now the target stick projects just a bit beyond the back of the vehicle. Photo 4: Success! The parakeet pushes the vehicle.

Game Instructions # For Skillful Birds: Tube and Tunnel Exercise

For parakeets, tunnels and tubes are nothing out of the ordinary. In the open, they investigate all sorts of tiny holes to see if they are suitable for nesting holes when the environmental conditions are suitable for breeding. Especially with females, there is no holding back. You can make good use of this curiosity in a sports exercise for parakeets.

DIFFICULTY

★ ★ ★ ★ ★

MATERIALS

Several cardboard or foam rubber pipes, 4 to 6 inches (10–15 cm) in diameter, treats, target stick

First turn the tube over, then walk through it; for lively, experienced players this poses no problem!

Clear off the table on which you want to practice, and stand a short tube up on the table. It is a good idea to start with a tube of fairly small diameter because it can be tipped over more easily. Hold the tip of the target stick on the rim of the tube. When the parakeet bites the stick, give it a treat (photo 1). Next, hold the stick over the tube so that the parakeet has to stretch a little to reach the stick. Soon it will bite the rim of the tube instead of the stick (photo 2). The eventual goal of the exercise is for the parakeet to pull on the tube at the same time it pulls its beak back and to tip it slightly (photo 3). At first you can help a little with this and tip the tube with your hand so that the parakeet experiences success (photo 4). However, sometimes the tube should remain upright so that the bird understands that the only way to get a treat is to tip the tube over. By the third time, the tube should fall over so that the little bird doesn't get frustrated and want to quit the training exercise. This learning step can last a very long time, and it requires lots of patience on your part. At first, many parakeets are frightened when the tube suddenly tips over, and they fly away. In such cases, you can support the tube with your hand and guide it over slowly. Once the parakeet understands the exercise, set up several tubes so that the parakeet learns to tip them over routinely. Of course, there should be a little treat after every strenuous effort!

Through the Tube!

Now take a tube with a larger diameter that the parakeet can walk through easily. Again, begin with the target training and coax the parakeet to the tipped-over tube. If the parakeet follows the target stick reliably, hold the stick so that it protrudes toward the parakeet (photo 5). Now slowly draw the target stick into the tube so that the parakeet is lured ever closer to the tube (photo 6). Don't forget to reward the bird with a treat when it touches the tip of the target stick. Now coax your training partner right through the tube with the target stick (photo 7). Of course, the little bird must get an especially big treat at the other end, for it has cooperated marvel-

ously. If the tube moves when the parakeet is walking through it, either support it with your hand or with two braces on the sides.

Work on this part of the exercise until the parakeet walks through the tube on command, even without the target stick. Now you can place a second and even a third tube after the first one to create a regular course. You can even choose tubes with a smaller diameter so the bird has to exert a little more effort to scramble through.

Photo 3: Now the parakeet pulls on the rim in such a way that the tube tips slightly.

Photo 1: The target stick lures the parakeet to the rim of the tube. Photo 2: If the parakeet bites the tube, it gets a treat. Photo 4: Eventually the bird tips the tube.

Photo 5: Hold the target stick through the tube so that it sticks out of the other side. Give praise when the parakeet bites the tip. Photo 6: Slowly draw the stick through the tube so that the bird follows it. If it bites the stick, give it another treat. Photo 7: Success! The parakeet's head emerges from the tube.

Freestyle for Advanced Performers

When everything works well, combine the two exercises. First give the parakeet a tube and let the bird tip it over. Reinforce with a treat and immediately coax the parakeet through the tube. Once the bird understands this exercise sequence, delay the confirmation for tipping the tube over until the parakeet goes completely through the tube. The goal of the exercise is for the parakeet to tip over several tubes and walk through them. Save the treat for the end. Such a complex exercise is made up of many steps, and the number of treats is continually reduced during the course of the training.

Game Instructions

Action-packed Skateboarding

Parakeets can be taught to use a skateboard, and many of them will eventually enjoy riding on one, as these birds are already comfortable moving along the ground in their natural habitat in their search for food; however, it may take some patience on your part to get them accustomed to this method of "transportation."

DIFFICULTY ★ ★ ★ ★ ★

MATERIALS
A miniature skateboard suitable for parakeets, a rubber stopper, treats

For birds with such a gift of flight, skateboarding surely is an unusual means of locomotion. A parakeet that is already used to training will approach the skateboard curiously, but a timid bird may ignore it at first. Coax your training partner up to the skateboard with a treat and let it eat calmly next to the skateboard (photo 1).

Now hold a piece of millet in such a way that the parakeet has to crane over the skateboard to reach it. As soon as it puts one foot onto the skateboard, give the bird lots of praise and give it a good treat (photo 2).

Important: You need to provide praise at the precise instant when the parakeet touches the board. If the skateboard rolls away without the bird when it is touched, initially hold it in place with a little chock such as a rubber eraser. Once the parakeet routinely steps onto the board, remove the chock so that the skateboard begins to roll.

Now give the bird praise with a treat only when the skateboard moves while it is standing on it with one foot (photo 3). Gradually increase the distance that the bird must ride in order to get a treat.

Readers are always advised to check with pet shop owners and veterinarians concerning special characteristics or needs of their birds.

Addresses

American Federation of Aviculture
P.O. Box 91717
Austin, TX 78709
www.afabirds.org

American Budgerigar Society
www.abs1.org

Budgerigar Association of America
www.budgerigarassociation.org

An Internet search will reveal many state parakeet organizations.

Questions About Keeping Parakeets

Pet shop personnel and veterinarians are good individuals to consult for answers to your questions.

Books

Birmelin, Immanuel. *My Parakeet.* Hauppauge, NY: Barron's Educational Series, Inc., 2009.

Davids, Angela. *Budgies: A Guide to Caring for Your Parakeet.* Irvine, California: BowTie Press, 2006.

Niemann, Hildegard. *Budgerigars.* Hauppauge, NY: Barron's Educational Series, Inc., 2008.

Siino, Betsy Sikoro. *The Essential Parakeet.* New York, NY: Wiley Publishing, Inc., 1998.

Wolter, Annette. *The Parakeet Handbook.* Hauppauge, NY: Barron's Educational Series, Inc., 2000.

Parakeets on the Internet

Practical tips and information on care, feeding, and health of parakeets, plus useful books, addresses of breeders, and associations can be found on these websites.

www.budgiemania.com

www.budgieplace.com

www.budgies.org

www.boaf.com/article_2.htm

www.talkbudgies.com

Home page with photos and ideas on foraging and habitat improvement for parakeets: *www.feathersandforage.co.uk/*

Live cam of parakeets: *www.sandman.com/birdcast.htm*

Information about poisonous plants can be found at:

http://birds.about.com/od/livingwithabird/tp/Holiday-Plants-Toxic-To-Pet-Birds.htm

http://birds.about.com/b/2007/12/21/toxic-and-safe-plants-and-trees.htm

http://www.birdsnways.com/articles/plntstox.htm

Important Note

Sick Parakeets: If your bird shows symptoms of disease, take it to an avian veterinarian immediately. **Danger of Infection:** Only a few parakeet diseases are communicable to humans. Advise your doctor of your contact with animals. This applies especially in the case of flulike illnesses. Allergies and Asthma: Many people experience allergic reactions to feathers and feather dust. If you are unsure whether you will be affected by this, consult with your doctor before buying a parakeet.

Acknowledgments

The author and publisher are grateful to Mrs. Maisch and her parakeets for her support during the photo shoots, to Karl-Heinz Lambert for the outdoor photos, to the Rübenach Corp. (*www.volierenbau.de*), and to the Wagner Parrot Paradise (*www.parrotshop.de*) for making aviaries, cages, and toys available. Margareta Bindert and Sven Fischer thank the author and the publisher for the planning and construction of the outdoor setup.

First edition for the United States, its territories and dependencies, and Canada published in 2013 by Barron's Educational Series, Inc.

First edition translated from the German by Eric A. Bye, M.A., C. T.

Original title of the book in German is *Spiel- und Wohnideen für Wellensittiche.*

© Copyright 2011 by Gräfe und Unzer Verlag, GmbH, Munich.   G|U

All inquiries should be addressed to:
Barron's Educational Series, Inc.
250 Wireless Boulevard
Hauppauge, New York 11788
www.barronseduc.com

Library of Congress Catalog Card No. 2012034651

ISBN: 978-1-4380-0207-1

Library of Congress Cataloging-in-Publication Data
Niemann, Hildegard.
    [Spiel- und Wohnideen für Wellensittiche. English]
    Games and house design for parakeets / Hildegard Niemann ; translated from the German by Eric A. Bye. — First edition for the United States, its territories and dependencies, and Canada.
        pages cm
    Translation of the author's Spiel- und Wohnideen für Wellensittiche.
    Includes bibliographical references and index.
    ISBN: 978-1-4380-0207-1
 1. Budgerigar—Housing. 2. Budgerigar—Training.
3. Play behavior in animals. I. Title
SF473.B8N53713   2013
636.6'864—dc23   2012034651

The Author

Hildegard Niemann has a degree in biology and is a freelance consultant on parrot behavior. She advises owners of all kinds of parrots and parakeets about behavior, ownership, and feeding. She writes articles for magazines. She has had several books published, too.

The Photographer

Oliver Giel specializes in nature and animal photography and, along with his partner, Eva Scherer, he handles photo production for books, magazines, calendars, and advertisements. You can find more of his photos at *www.tierfotograf.com.*

All photos in this book are by **Oliver Giel**, with the exception of: **Karl-Heinz Lambert**, page 6. All illustrations in this book are by **Claudia Schick**.

Printed in China
9 8 7 6 5 4 3 2 1

1 A daily free flight is essential for long-distance fliers like parakeets. Getting them back into the aviary will be no problem with a little specific training. Please note: It is advised that you clip the wings of your bird to limit its ability to fly at full speed and, thus, potentially suffer injury.

2 Parakeets need sleep, too. In addition to an ample midday break, ten hours of quiet nighttime sleep in a dark room is important to keep the birds even-tempered. Lack of sleep leads to aggressiveness and apathy. A curtain in front of the aviary will provide a quiet environment for your birds.

10 Tips for Success and Happy Parakeets

As offspring of the wilderness, parakeets are undemanding birds. However, you should meet their most important requirements and needs to keep them feeling content.

3 As prey animals, parakeets are sensitive to a lack of safe hiding places. Do not place the aviary right in front of a window, but always in a light corner of the room. Your parakeets can learn to trust you only when they feel protected and secure.

4 Parakeets feel secure only in the company of other birds; this is in harmony with their natural way of life. So never keep just one parakeet, but rather at least two.